HE PAVES THE ROAD WITH IRON BARS

poems

Caroline Knox

ALSO BY CAROLINE KNOX

The House Party

To Newfoundland

Sleepers Wake

A Beaker: New and Selected Poems

HE PAVES THE ROAD WITH IRON BARS

poems

Caroline Knox

VERSE PRESS

AMHERST, MASSACHUSETTS

Published by Verse Press

Copyright © 2004 by Caroline Knox

Library of Congress Cataloging-in-Publication Data

Knox, Caroline.
    He paves the road with iron bars : poems / Caroline Knox.
    p. cm.
    ISBN 0-9723487-6-x (alk. paper)
    I. Title.
PS3561.N686H4 2004
811'.54—DC22

                                        2003019293

Cover photo: Bettmann/Corbis
Designed and composed by Elizabeth Knox
Display set in Copperplate. Text set in Minion.

9   8   7   6   5   4   3   2   1

First Edition

Contents

Acknowledgments

Poems in this collection have appeared in
Boston Review, Chiaroscuro, Denver Quarterly,
Electronic Poetry Review, Fence, Fine Madness, How 2, LIT,
Mississippi Review (New York School of Poets Issue),
New American Writing, No Roses Review, Northeast Journal,
Poets On, Slope, and *Sycamore Review.*

The author is grateful for a Harvard University Visiting Fellowship
(2002–2003), and for the kindness of three professors:
Laurel Thatcher Ulrich and Catherine Corman, historians,
and Jennifer Roberts, art historian.

HE PAVES THE ROAD
WITH IRON BARS

His Heart

His heart keeps him awake while he's asleep.
He listens to his heart while he falls asleep in bed.
His artificial heart gives him insomnia.
As long as I can hear the sound, I know I'm here.

His heart keeps him alive while he's asleep.
My heart helps me to sleep while I'm alive.
Oh, patient, this Valentine is for you.

I had no choice, I knew that I was dying.
We are trying to survive. We are standing on the shoulders
of the makers of the heart while we lie on our back in bed.
They walk with their hearts on their sleeves and their noses to
    the grindstone.
He listens to his heart while he falls asleep at night.

Oh, Valentine, this contraption is for you,
device of the scared, the sacred heart.
It feels heavy to me—it makes a constant whir
which keeps me awake when I'm trying to get to sleep.
It has no heartbeat, only this constant whir.

JOHN SINGER SARGENT

We read John Wheelwright's poems and John Mason Brown's essays
   and John
Philip Sousa's memoirs. Then I read John Peale Bishop and John
Malcolm Brinnin. Then a little John Greenleaf Whittier and John
Quincy Adams's *Amistad* letters, and John
Bernard Myers's exquisite essay, "The Other," about animals in art.
   I next read *John
Singleton Copley,* by Jules Prown, and then together we (my friends
   and I, not Dr. Prown) read *Émile, par Jean-
Jacques Rousseau, avec notre lexique tout près de nous.* John
James Audubon we next read part of in the great Library of America
   edition. John
Henry Newman's *Callista* I read some of. It takes place in a sewer.
   And Burns's "John
Anderson, my Jo, John."

We read *The Singer
of Tales,* by Milman Parry and Albert P. Lord, and re-read the tales of
   Isaac Bashevis Singer;
we read in the Golden Retriever about *Annie Hall*'s hero, Alvy Singer.
The book group read *Writings on an Ethical Life,* by Peter Singer.
I leafed through the score of *Die Meistersinger
Von Nürnburg.* We read aloud about Julia A. Moore, the Sweet Singer
of Michigan. We read everything we could get our hands on by
   Arthur Schlesinger,
Jr. I read what he wrote about Kissinger

and about Sargent
Shriver as head of the Peace Corps and the OEO, and we read aloud
from the sleeve of *Sergeant
Pepper's Lonely Hearts Club Band.* We read *The Story of Margaretta,*
by Judith Sargent
Murray, and considered *Charles P. Sargent
and the Arnold Arboretum,* by S. B. Sutton. We printed stuff out from
the website of marvelous Phil Silvers, who played Sergeant
Bilko on TV. And finally, we checked out *British and American
Utopian Literature,* by Lyman Tower Sargent;
Asking about Zen, by Jiho Sargent;
and *Bounded Rationality in Macroeconomics,* by Thomas P. Sargent.

Barrel-Vault

The recipe for its vernacular façade
is $\frac{\pi r^2}{2}$. A semi-cylinder
pictured with tectonic ventilators
in Volume I of a government publication,
Building the Navy's Bases in World War II
(History of the Bureau of Yards and Docks
and the Civil Engineer Corps, 1941–
1945), the quonset hut
is in fact a barrel-vault, before which stand

its edifying crew, their work complete, preserved
on film: shiny and smiling, *comme il faut,*
yet slightly embarrassed. Charlayne Hunter-Gault
remembers going to school in one of these
"hot, airless, quonset-hut-type structures
on an unpaved, dusty, red-clay lot in the middle
of nowhere." And somewhere in western France
you can look up at the barrel-vault of Poitiers
cathedral, which its master builder spelt

(if he wrote, on blue vellum, as nones was ringing)
Poictiers, and pronounced Poyk Teers. Pre-quonset,
the barrel-vault is the habitation of shadow,
and you can see and hear the haunting mirror
and echo elsewhere as well: the counterpart
of the barrel-vault is the canyon, a place of wind
and drought. Poitiers is to the mistral
as Canyon de Chelly to the chinook,
and like all barrel-vaults is a monument

overbuilt by over two hundred percent,
whose likely ancestor was a working drainage
system in ancient Rome which actually worked
efficiently, and whose vault approximated
eight hundred feet in length by ten across,
something useful that hadn't been there before,
as $\frac{\pi r^2}{2}$ became the roof
over H_2O. Less lofty than these instances,
but nevertheless vernacular problem-solving:

my neighbor coops his chickens with this shape,
with galvanized and corrugated metal
(like half a storm-drain conduit on its side
intended to keep rain out of people's cellar
windows). The farmer rotates the metal object
ninety degrees and bolts it to leftover plywood.
Beneath, the chickens shelter in a barrel-
vault, and all the eggs they lay are blue,
as blue as the ether over Poitiers.

But I. M. Pei and Partners bear the bell.
They connect the old part of the Museum
of Fine Arts in Boston with the new part,
including the Gund Gallery; they connect
these elements by a gasket made of glass,
crunchy-looking cells in a barrel-vault design
brimming with light—a long, translucent, inclusive
way of holding onto new and old at once
forever and still remaining beautiful.

Boot and Bonnet

He picked me up in the vaunted car.
When Milton wrote, "The gilded car

of day," he meant this car, a NASCAR
reject, with a broccoli elastic holding the tailpipe on the car.

"'Special' is such a general word," he of the car
allowed to me, dreaming at the car-

wash. *Car
and Driver* is his car

magazine. In Connecticut they have Connecticar,
which brings you borrowed books in a car.

A worn Bokhara lines the trunk of the car.
Brits say boot for trunk, and bonnet for the front of the car.

CAFÉ MARY ROWLANDSON

We all foregathered at the speak,
even him with the paperclip on the end of his given name.
Crats were there, but not Muggletonians.
It's an honor to be asked, but a pain to go.

First, this. "The boots of the men CLMP/
On the boards of the bridge"—physics for poets.
"Oh, [Taxasoit]*," cried I,
using the nominative of direct address,
"the English are lying doggo at Hagminster.
They did not wet their foot.
Their houses, which shine, are jackstraws."
Pouncer was there with Taxasoit.
Yes, Pouncer was with him.

I can remember the time when I was
scrupulous to note
a "protracture of antique imagerie"
A narrative of the troubles?
A history of the war?

But now it is other ways with me
down at the Café Mary Rowlandson
(The Mess of Pease, The Hoof Soup; Bear, Pone).
We were not yet ready to get ransomed.
We were not yet ready to go home.

EASTER

Jelly Bird Egg, the presence of a soup of beans
sends the consumer, can and all. Ice cream
resists chews by that very consumer by aggregate of sugar pustules.

Jelly Bird Egg, made by Psychotherapy Chicken,
full of willingness to doubt self, others, and be pleased,
here at the Snazzatorium, to apprehend
just such a Jelly Bird Egg as God rolled from her or his mind for you.

I Speak out of the *Exeter Book*

in a "mildly frightening way…usurping the human
prerogative of speech." A parallelogram
like the deflected element in cutwork
(an embroidery technique), I ask you who I am. Diane Glancy
said, "These letters can be read as holes in the text."
You can look through them. What is there. Fabio and Charro.

The hole is a gate. I am a field like a sieve.
I may have been made by Hwaetbert, Abbot of Wearmouth,
and friend of the Venerable Bede, who invented the rosary,
or Hildegarde von Binghamton, maybe a SUNY grad student?

SPAM Haiku Found Epic

SPAM Ingredients:
Pork and Ham, Salt, Water, Su-
gar, Sodium Ni-

trate. U.S. INSPECT-
ED AND PASSED BY DEPARTMENT
OF AGRICULTURE

Serving Suggestion
SPAMBLED™ EGG MUFFIN
SEE RECIPE ON

BACK Hormel Foods Net
WT. 12 OZ. (340
g) Copyright Hor-

mel Foods recycla-
ble aluminum Nu-
trition Facts Serv. Size

2 OZ. (56
g) Servings per container
6 Calories 1-

70 Fat Cal.
140 Amount/Serving
%DV* Tot-

al Fat 16g
25% Sat. Fat
16g 30

% Cholest. 4-
0mg   13%
Sodium 7-

50mg
31%   Amount/
Serving   %D

V*   Total Carb. 0
g 0%   Fiber
0%   Su-

gars 0%   Pro-
tein 7g   Vita-
min A 0%

Vitamin C 0
%   Calcium
0%   I-

ron 2%   *Per-
cent Daily Values (DV)
are based on a 2,-

000 calorie
diet. Packed by Hormel Foods
Corporation, Cor-

porate Office, Aus
tin, Minnesota 55-
912   SPAMBLED™

EGG MUFFIN   EASY SPAM-
BLED™   EGG MUFFINS   Slice
SPAM® Luncheon Meat in-

to 4–6 square slice-
s.   Broil or heat in skillet.
Scramble 4–6

eggs. Layer eggs, meat
and one slice American
cheese between toasted

English muffin halves.
Heat 10 seconds in micro-
wave. Makes 4–6

SPAMBLED™ Egg
Muffins. To order SPAM™
™ Merchandise and

Apparel call 1-
800-LUV-SPAM   Product
questions and comments,

please call 1-800
523-4635.
SPAM and SPAMBLED are

trademarks of Hormel
Foods Corporation SPAM FULL-
Y COOKED, READY TO

EAT—COLD OR HOT.   SLICED
SPAM LUNCHEON MEAT; Cut into
8–10 slices; arrange

in baking dish. Spread
with favorite sauce or glaze.
BAKE at 42-

5°F for
10–12 minutes, or MIC-
ROWAVE at High for

2 ½ min-
utes, or PAN-FRY slices un-
til browned on both sides.

3760-
0   13872
Here ends the epic.

Quatrains by Hester Mulso
(1729–1764)

"The *old Yahoos* were a thousand times
more wicked and unreasonable
than a little Yahoo would be." "The
Harlowes bade Clarissa be

good and consequently happy."
"Fathers are taught by Bishop
Hall (I don't love that Bishop
Hall, why did you quote him?)

to believe their children *goods* and
chattels." "A tyrant master to his servant:
'You thought! how *dare* you to think? Do I
keep you to think?'" "I am ready

to subscribe to all that Pufendorf
says, with this proviso: that
the filial duty be owing to those
who perform the parental duty."

"Nothing will induce me to design
an ending for *Sir Charles Grandison.*"
"You cannot be too conversant with the
Psalms, a continuous feast." "Avoid

of all things intimacy with those
of low birth and education." "Affection
is not like a portion of freehold land."
"In the case of real injuries, express

a noble and generous kind of anger."
"Youth may pursue wealth with all the
rapacity of an old usurer." Dr. Johnson
chose a quatrain from Hester's "Ode to Stella"

to illustrate the entry for "Quatrain"
in *A Dictionary of the English Language*:

"Say, Stella, what is love, whose fatal pow'r
Robs virtue of content, and youth of joy?
What nymph or goddess in a luckless hour
Disclos'd to light the mischief-making boy?"

Jane's Birthday Party

"Why should we—anybody—," said you,
"require written things to have content?"
You went
on to say, "We—anyone—don't object
(in fact, we *expect*
art, painted, to be abstract,
don't we?) to canvas
and stone that are without."

"And look at Louise." "*You* look at her."
"Not that one. The other."

Whereas with a written down thing,
if style alone—well—nervous making
not to have goal and so on,
nor something to take home, like a balloon.

Which figment superscribes your very
good health and merry
days, requiring content, cake, and surprise too.

COIN-FACED MAN

Coin-faced man, I am calibrated for numismatics.
Do you have a yen for the real?

Turns out, "[C]oins, although they confirm history,"
said Dr. Blenkinsop, "rarely correct it.
Numismatics is an offspring of sculpture."

For an obverse monarch or a tree,
the octagonal die is strikable;
struck or cast, bite on the coin to see if it's a slug.
We played Honeysuckle Stoopnagle with the coin-faced man.

Turns out, Dr. Blenkinsop is an old boy in *The Doctor's Dilemma*,
and Honeysuckle Stoopnagle is nothing but Hide the Thimble.
But man-faced coin, four bits—it's JFK
on a scumbled field from the Philly mint.
They belted him with a Margoliouth.
Woe to consequences so hardened!
Chicago, San Francisco papers please copy.

Sound and Light

The difference between the phone and the remote
is the phone has a little aerial on it;
if you want TV, use one; if you want people
use the other. The phone has the alphabet
in trifids. You don't have an aerial
on the remote. There's a phone
in the car, but no TV.

I have to have a book to really read.
Sometimes I email a blank screen.
These words were given to me to say:
sound navigation and ranging; light amplification by simulation
    of radiation.

Clique Ici

Fill out the form on line; complete the waiver
application; follow the links the way
the prompts instruct you. Enter your PIN,
Benevolent and Protective Order of Elks.

Log on, log in; if you're a Brit, fill *up*
the form. Oh, Mothers Against Drunk Driving,
fill out the form on line and click on Save
As. Oh, click on Save, Society of Jesus.

Rotarians, Hide Balloons. Jaycees, Shut Down.
Portuguese Holy Ghost Club, go to the web,
and Keyword Orville Redenbacher, Browse or Search.
Provide your screen name, Healthy Androscoggin.

Type in your password, Loyal Order of Moose.
Patrons of Husbandry, oh, Sign On, Sign On
Again. Click Set Up, Medieval Colloquium
of the Lehigh Valley, and Wheelabrator Frye—
print out this page, which will act as your receipt.

A Fuzzy Map of England on King Lear's Back

Don't you think it's a weird usage
to call the paper contract an instrument—
marks and seals which you could tear across
(not that I'm going to—I'm keeping this one).

There are ribbons even on some of the
instruments, like clothing
(with a bright wax disc notarized)
in cursive uncials and subjunctives.

Or it almost sounds like a mandolin
plucked from the heart, a blunt instrument.
But nobody is going to take anything more
away from you now. He has spoken. I hope I'm right.

Freddy as Sweeney

A man holding egad a bumbershoot
walks along a boundary, the Imaginot Line.
Gentlemen, a bunfight this ack emma at the beanery.
This is *Friederichsschmerz*, O Flintstone
(head in hands, missing at the Somme).

I say out loud the facts I know
about T. S. Eliot as I do every year
to the class, I mean the redoubtable
hero Sweeney. Freddy recommends
this etymology to Dr. Puffkin, who resides
at Puffkin-le-Willowes, with his wife of a thousand years.

PROTHALAMIUM

Here is the cairn of gifts: in tailored silver paper
with hospital corners; wired gauze ribbon
effects never to be so neatly arranged again,
probably. How thoughtful!

Dear Field-Marshal and Mrs. Montgomery, Thank you for the
    beautiful present from Marshall Field's.
Dear Field-Marshal and Mrs. Montgomery, Thank you for the
    beautiful present from Montgomery Ward.

Here is the pledge at the rehearsal dinner:
"With love in my heart I offer you this toast."
The uncle presents two slices of Pepperidge Farm.

This is the knot of marzipan rosettes for the cake.
This is the knot of ivory rosettes on the bride's chignon.
This is her handsome bridegroom.

That guest's hat looks like a miner's lamp.
That guest's dress is made of Putron.

Here is the gift of cairns: a pair of expensive, inquisitive terriers
ready to adore you—are you ready for them?

At Dawn, Iris Appeared to Me

She read the paper while I drank my orange
juice. Of course she read the Yellow
Pages. I was green
with envy at her deep blue
raiment, her violet
eyes. The radio opined about Brown
v. Board of Ed. I got out my Black

and Decker grass trimmer, crimson
in hue, and annihilated the vermilion
poison ivy, but spared the wild mustard
along the viridian
path beneath the azure
dome, Tyrian
toward dusk and then of course chestnut,
basalt.

Beets,
salmon,
lemons,
avocado,
blueberries,
eggplant,
liverwurst
—these we chowed down on, and of course beluga.

It was a tony evening: we discussed *The Red
and the Black, A Clockwork Orange,
The Yellow
Wallpaper, Sir Gawain and the Green
Knight, The Blue
Angel, The Color Purple*
of course, *John Brown's
Body*, and—before this Iris took off at midnight—as I say, *The Red
and the Black.*

Gnome Acrostic

Adages were a staple of poetry
before the Common Era,
since the fall of
Troy VIIA in about 1200.
Recent sayings continue the trend:
"As Vermont goes, so goes the nation";
"Can't we get
those guys on RICO?"
   "Listen,
   your mother wears army boots,"
   replied the gnome.
   I'm a denizen of Ortshire—
   Cui bono?"

He Paves the Road with Iron Bars

"Get into the railroad car,"
wrote Waldo Emerson in 1832,
"and the Ideal Philosophy
takes place at once.
Matter seems compromised."

Emerson was a *bel inconnu*
who "snickered at embarrassing moments."
He had "the mouse in his chest." It was TB.
The doctor was called Dr. Frisbie.

Waldo "had no taste for comedy,"
wrote Gay Wilson Allen in the biography,
and disliked complex trope.
In Rome, he thought Pope
Gregory XVI was "millinery
and imbecility."

Nature grew slowly out
of letter
and ser-
mon and jour-
nal, as when he saw "a trail of glowing cinder
beside the track;
the hissing steam made the traveler
stand back."
Passing freight cars full of timber
"darted by like trout."

Current history,
art history,
and historiography
address material culture and see

lies and myths, "objects and stories" in a thing
such as a tea-kettle, which
by contrast is also
for Waldo
Emerson a loco-
motive. Where he wrote, "Hitch
your wagon to a star,"
"wagon" may have meant "railway car"
(OED
5b),
while "trees and men whiz by
you as fast as the leaves of a dictionary."
Harriet Martineau
wrote of Waldo,
"In coaches or steamboats or
any where else that
he saw people of colour
ill-used, he did what
he could and said what he thought."
Yet Duane
Coltharp calls Emerson's train
"a celebration of capitalist power."
This detail
can be found through
libarts.wsu
.edu
/English/Archive/Journals/ESQ
/Index.hotmail.

I sat in my auditor's seat listening
to Laurel Thatcher
Ulrich, Cather-
ine Corman, and Jennifer
Roberts holding
forth on background to all this. I did the reading.
("Objects and stories" above is Ulrich's coining.)

Waldo had a
"bias toward the concrete,"
wrote Robert D. Richardson, Jr., in the biography;
in the subject's words, the
"din and craft of the street."
In Liverpool, he "went
to the railroad and saw
Rocket and Goliath and Pluto
and Firefly,
the vulcanian generation,"
he said in Journal Q
(1832).
In this nation,
where whistles soon blew
twice a day for Waltham and for
Boston, the first engine names were Best
Friend, West
Point, and E. L. Miller,
although the cowcatcher patent,
#8996, wasn't until 1852.

As it were a house, a canal, a statue, a picture,
here in America, the railroad creates
"an
American
sentiment,"
Waldo wrote; the solid
enough
ground of *Nature*
—we can't get out
of it—is stuff:
"He paves the road with iron bars";
but this material, or Commodity,
alone is "mean and squalid";
while "the mind is a steam-shop where power
is generated no matter for what uses."
And, wrote Lee

Rust Brown, "The transparency
can see
through
the object to
a whole of which the thing
is a fragment,"
as Carlyle was shown the railway cars:
rolling stock: flatbeds, passengers, cabooses—
flanged vehicles along
a stream of worker song
all day
"for the sugar in my tay"
by the destitute. "These are our poems," Carlyle said.
Indeed by 1849 Waldo
under duress
of writing lecture and essay
himself surmised
he had on the terrain
of *Nature* become a train:
"I am a literary runner and Lyceum Express."

The Graph of a Thing

You better not, chickie, and her rising warning voice
takes on the electronic note, it's nothing but the sireen and dogs
    reacting after all.
Perfectly OK now, seriously, it might be on TV, like a dessert
    commercial
but no grains of gelatin on the counter *there*.
Which those townships seem to be a kind of eye's autograph
made in a newspaper dot picture, close up but broken down, of an
    accident by a building (that's urban haiku mix).
A bike trip would be getting off, although the map would get paper
    fatigue with you *on* it.
The graph of a thing fits in your hand, glove with stump and strings
    attached.
You can't have mere quenching of fashion. Or theory anchoring
    practice
by interior-decorator drawing pins, ornamented by little seeds and
    pods closed in lucite.
Who is to expect a snazzy still-life on the inside of a drawing pin, for
    Pete's sake?
Causality by any standards provisional and ancillary, deep thoughts,
    deep thoughts.
Pin's divine correlates grommet and sprocket rubbed with gasoline,
    ergo hurl light.
Massive hills circumvent voluptuousness, fear and pleasure explode
    out of the commons of machines.

Yule Log

Please know that in the eyes of the stable's beasties
there is a poor-born baby boy reflected, or that's what they say,
under a pergola made of balsa wood, a thin
and friable tinder, sir, so watch out in an overheated room
full of graven images. Praise to the fin
of the ICHTHOS, since these are creatures who do
what they're told. The stork itself should be found
lurking about somewhere here on the Chinese
screen with *Blessed is the fruit of thy womb*
but the stork might be Dutch or Flemish even.
        Keep the holiday
                Don't order me around
and anyway who could take it away from you?
so close to what used to be celebrated as the Feast of Stephen.

The Loafers of the Sea

This is Mudguard the beautiful
wreathed along the fusts as usual

Jane walked up to you and said,
Timeo Danaos et dona ferentes

Some "pineapple claim" quaking with juice
Tears of the ahem votive moose

Conduits are responsive. Our sneakers empty.
The dark loon in Bird World is the complement

In Mudguard, in Mudguard, all the time pard-girt treen.
Oh god it's Jane again who cries
Ars sine scientia nihil est

Kenneth Koch wrote, "What dialect are you speaking,
you, wearing the loafers of the sea?" What did he mean?

We stayed at the swell *Hôtel de Ville*
I picked up a heavy book
Les livres disponibles, par Victor Hugo

The houses are haunted by Lanz nightgowns
Some are green, or purple with green rings
Or green with yellow rings or yellow with blue rings

All of them are strange. See the nice ducky, operator.
Farewell to Yaz, what ho, Harley Street bat!
"Ten years younger than fifteen minutes ago."

HALF MOON

The *Halve Maen* came up.
Speech was full of *aa* and *je, van* and *van der.*

Then, Maria Hasbrouck married Abraham Hardenberg.
Maps said: *Waranawakong.*
A ship's manifest said: "Five hundred otter and two hundred beaver
    skins, for twenty thousand guilders."
Next, Anneke Schoonmaker married Hendrikus Jansen.

The *zee* was full of salt and chop—what a surprise;
the salt air was full of quaint *rinkelbel* chimes. The sleighs
"flew with great swiftness, and some were so furious
that they would turn out of the way for none but a loaded cart!"

"My great-grandfather spoke Dutch
so he could tell the dominie what to do."

Next, maps said: *Novum Eboracum.*

THE DUEL

The seconds, the brushed business clothes, and brace of pistols
out of velvet bags, and the traveled eye of the opponent whose
   thrifty breath
is like yours, isn't it? all these are—why did you ask him?—
optional and decorative to prevent a blunder
and he has a maverick coral heart to fight about a woman
or a contract or a point of honor; what got you into this
tenuous hold on film if it is film
to make him ask you back for drinks to a bleached terrace?
One of the pistols is a cigar lighter, or holds catsup; the other soda
   water.
The little formal man is the gardener's brother who is laughing
and is completely responsible for the topiary—
awful little sounds as if every clay tile
were being shattered in a nameless duchy.
Enter then you, my friend, something to say for yourself,
something to indicate the commodiousness of air as he splashes
   vermouth on your boots.

Think: it took several badgers to make his moustache
And was their sacrifice to a good end? were they "spared"?
And why not fight the gardener, who speaks no English.
Why fight? It is a plum, he explains, and a present from a Chinese
   doctor
whom I assisted once over a hurdle, *prunus boadiceana*
I think it is, ornamental and slow-growing.
Isn't it more admirable to confront your own interior
where the cilia of the esophagus defer to the stomach, even in the
   case of powdered sugar?
But isn't it? but the shadow on the plantings now black and jagged,
   total awe,
with the sun creeping away from rescuing you and
a slippery trumpet sounds for your indecision to get over with

interrupted by several paid teenagers in their early twenties
on leave of absence from high school attending college,
to join hands with that gardener's brother and then the cackling of
    you all! the hammering of hearts and terrace-jumping!

Common Place

"A riverboat
ferry is efficient to carry
apricots northward in Siberia";
so she said who was part of the convoy and shared passage.

"The last glacier was not so long ago.
There are the scratches."
So James Schuyler in 1970.

A commonplace book
made out of commonplace books in Zone 6:
a man is reading *De Rorem Natura*, by Ned Rorem.
A woman is reading the *Journal of Fonzarelli Studies.*

(Nearby a lady in a leghorn hat
puts away chowder with her "world-class boyfriend,"
Orlando di Lasso, of the spaghetti westerns.
They turn and turn on the parquet
Able   Baker   Charlie   Dog
to the New Rhythm and Blues Quartet.)

He: So We To
         Cha Ri Ho
         Ou Li Po

She: Li-Po? (and procrastinating the GRE:)
         Man = sofa   Guy = Davenport
         Sursum corda   *tiramisú*

He: Light planes hot-dogging among the Perseids!
         "Illness is not a tragedy, but a commonplace event";
         so Tom Andrews in *Codeine Diary.*

She: Abcissa of motive-project vector.

He: De facto Feng shui and Karaoke Festschrift.

And she is wearing her lonely cartouche:
"RIP Fritters Summer '98.
Not even my beagle.
Hardly even beagle."

Lost Cows

Oh, no—"Lost Cows at 148 Narrows Road"
(even people who live here get lost):
a corrugated cardboard sign in marker pen,
nailed to a phone pole, and people are out looking
for bossy and her bull-calf lost from mother
moping and moaning at 148;
and more lost cows are lowing and following.
Oh, cows; oh, no—oh, no news of lost cows.
And other folks have gone out looking for the lost—
for bossy and bull calf parted from mother,
like lost people moping and moaning, *memento mori,* a e i o u.
Now now, oh crowd from Narrows Road: those cows
are crossing The Narrows now to high and fallow
ground, love-lorn bossy and love-lost bull-calf,
gone from each other. Oh, they're looking
around, those cows, that bull-calf
looking for mom, that mom losing her
bull-calf, mourning, and other cows too. They're crossing brooks,
they're fording The Narrows, trying to get home. Their owners
looking for them, moping and moaning,
behooving these lines to end with an alexandrine,
as from sorrow and loss in aunt-like steps all these cows come home.

Glassworks

They were boiling pans of gunge to eventually make soap, and
　　supposedly there were "towering shard-rucks of spoiled pots,"
in the early Wedgewood manufactories. Keir the Scotsman was
　　responsible for a lot of this:
he isolated slowly cooled glass crystals,
that looked like acorn squash, snowflakes, and bathtub scrubbers.
　　He gave Wedgewood the recipe
for the raw materials of flint glass to make a standard thick elegant
　　pottery glaze.

But England's first glassmakers were Continental immigrants,
　　migrants, whose routes have been traced "in cullet-heaps and
　　broken-down furnaces,
and by their names, often mutilated, on parish registers," while
　　stateside one of the Glass Flowers will occasionally burst into
　　smithereens. Cotton Mather
yearned to know more about the spontaneous craziness: "What
　　should be the meaning in the broken windows for us?"—in 1695.
Glass is full of palimpsests like forgotten words,
much as, when I was a kid, skating on a backwater of the Charles
　　one day I rattled across the hobnail white ice to clear black
and looking down in alarm saw a sodden and frozen rowboat lying
　　on the bottom,
another world parallel and lost, drowned but also petrified, so I was
　　petrified too.

And to scuttle this poem, see more glass. All -mongers and -wrights
　　should go to glass class
and learn to make work stark or ornamented with a fillip, powers
　　employed and exerted;
what about a Dorkington Cranberry/Marigold *épergne*, highly
　　sought after! Or cobalt

liners that nestle in salt cellars, preventing oxidization. They use
sand and soda and lime.
You can make your own windowpanes full of warts and bumps, of a
sophisticated lavender
—pierce your house with beveled grisaille: that's the boilerplate of
the trade, or the billingsgate—
make it like Ste. Chapelle, almost ninety percent pierced, a world
away from hands-on Enlightenment science projects.
You yourself can make fake onyx or jet, just by vastly increasing the
proportion of charcoal in the molten vortex.

Volunteer Lawyers for the Arts

I was in the Browsing Area of the Public Library
reading about the life of Pope Guilty III.
The Volunteer Lawyers for the Arts
were holding their Annual Meeting.
They showed me how to go © Common-Law Copyright.

I dwelt at 300 North Zeeb Road,
Ann Arbor, MI, 48106,
with University Microfilms.

There were the old cobblestones out the window,
and it was snowing on their rain.
Guilty wore a manhole cover by way of halo
—this is Public History.
Then it was *Stupor Mundi,* or Nap Time.

THE DAY OFF

The knight on his day off slept till ten
and walked around the house in his pajama bottoms

and then finally roped his roan horse
and took off through the peach orchard into the wilderness

My horse knows my name is Sir John
but he names me Oats Man

When the knight came to the fat spring brook
he swiped someone's canoe to cross it

A horse cannot fit in a canoe
so this one swam after, snorting at lilypads

Listen to you snort   said the knight
It is hot on the water   *I want my dinner*

My horse wants to be me
the way I want to be someone unknown

In a prescriptive shade the horse
grazed and the knight lolled with sandwiches

light seeded rye ritzily
stuffed with camembert, onions, and chicken

In sorrow no laziness not sorrow
beer in hand he sang this song

Now Ah'll be lo-ong gone in freedom tah-ah-ahm
and Ah'll see yew in the mornin' dew

who Ah leave behah-ah-ahnd
Let's stay in touch   *(Let's stay in touch)*

with the human race   with a lopin' lariat
and a long-gone trailsahd place

Now the song was boring to the singer
so he sank down in the deepest sleep

Winter fell on him as his dream
and the green air went gray above him

He looked in the land-locked brook and saw
girlfriends calling from the ocean

twigs in their romantically fishy hair
birds' wings and nests   *This state of things!*

land-locked calling with no sound
My birds! he shouted   *So stuck up!*

But the horse's dream went like this:
oats danced for him to oaten flutes

Oats fell in his world of nutrients
and their song fell on his sleekness like a comb

(Said oats stuck to his back in fact
like a winter coat in the waking world)

His dream recurred in his horse life
to be the balm of his athletic bones

Shivers in each of them shook off sleep
and left them in a warm twilight

Oh my horse your gravity
Is a sweet jitney in the late day

I know your name is Kentucky Bivouac
but I name you Air Impressionist

At home the knight soaked his sore feet and read
emails from his aunt in British Columbia

At home at home the horse re-embraced
the day off in the hectares of his mind

NODE WONK ISSUES

Node   wonk   node
Wonk   issues
Not duh! but huh? to stall for power
which is intellectual property, in so many words:
cries from the brain. See how you go,
with your exit strategy for gumboil magnetos
in the nerf quiche zone, dude

Zone of dearth, wonk node
Zone of issues, oh streaming postal one

NOTES

"His Heart." Several lines are quoted from an interview with Robert Tools, first recipient of the AbioCor artificial heart (Lawrence K. Altman, *New York Times*, August 22, 2001; A1, A16).

"Barrel-Vault." Jean Losinski, monographer of Poitiers cathedral, tells me that the monument has groin vaults only.

"Café Mary Rowlandson." Lines 18 and 19 are taken from Jill Lepore's work *The Name of War* (New York 1998, xvii, e. g.).

"I Speak out of the *Exeter Book*." The quotation is Michael Alexander's definition of the Anglo-Saxon riddle (*The Earliest English Poems*, Berkeley 1970; 125, 126). Diane Glancy's comment on Native American pictographs is from her novel *Pushing the Bear* (New York 1996).

"Quatrains by Hester Mulso." A group of sentences from Hester Mulso Chapone's prose works is arranged as quatrains (*Bluestocking Feminism*, Gary Kelly, General Editor. Vol. 3, Hester Mulso Chapone, ed. Rhoda Zuk. London; Brookfield VT, 1999).

"He Paves the Road with Iron Bars." In line 29, the phrase "objects and stories" is part of the subtitle of Laurel Thatcher Ulrich's book *The Age of Homespun* (New York 2001). Sam Knox provided a midrash on Commodity.

"Glassworks." The first two quotations are from Jenny Uglow, *The Lunar Men* (London 2002, 46). The third paraphrases the entry for 4/29/1695 in the *Diary of Samuel Sewall* (New York 1973).

ABOUT THE AUTHOR

Caroline Knox's books are *A Beaker: New and Selected Poems* (Verse Press 2002), *Sleepers Wake* (Timken 1994), and *To Newfoundland* and *The House Party* (Georgia 1989, 1984).

Her work has appeared in *American Scholar, American Voice, Boston Phoenix, Harvard, Massachusetts Review, New Republic, Paris Review, Ploughshares,* and *Poetry,* whose Bess Hokin Prize she has won.

She has received awards from the National Endowment for the Arts, the Massachusetts Cultural Council, the Yale/Mellon Visiting Faculty Program, the Fine Arts Work Center Senior Fellowship Program, the Ingram Merrill Foundation, and The Fund for Poetry. *He Paves the Road with Iron Bars* was completed on a Visiting Faculty Fellowship in affiliation with the Department of History at Harvard University, 2002–2003.

MATTHEW ROHRER
Satellite
A Green Light

STEVE SHAVEL
How Small Brides Survive in Extreme Cold

JAMES TATE
Dreams of a Robot Dancing Bee

DIANE WALD
The Yellow Hotel

JOE WENDEROTH
Letters to Wendy's

DARA WIER
Hat on a Pond

WWW.VERSEPRESS.ORG